DUCKIE COOKIE©
AND HER CIRCLE OF FRIENDS

FRAN GHADIMI

Illustrations by Craig Howarth

To order additional copies of this book, contact:
Xlibris
1-888-795-4274
www.Xlibris.com
Orders@Xlibris.com

ISBN: Softcover   978-1-4363-2242-3
         Hardcover   978-1-7960-7780-3
         EBook   978-1-7960-7781-0

Library of Congress Control Number: 2008901422

Print information available on the last page

Rev. date: 12/11/2019

  The sun was about to come up on the east side of the lake. The air was
clean and refreshing. The early morning breeze touched Duckie Cookie's
face. She opened her eyes. It was still very early to leave the bed. After all
it was a Saturday morning and folks do not wake up early. Her grandma
always told her the one who starts the day early will always finish the day
merrily. Aside from what her grandma said she always liked to go to bed
early and wake up early in the morning. In fact she was a morning animal.

She entered the lake and began to swim and play in the water. While she was swimming around in the lake she realized that she was not the only one there. Indeed, there were other early birds in the lake who started their day even earlier than she did. She swam and played in the water for a while. She totally enjoyed the start of her day.

On Saturday mornings Duckie Cookie always made her delicious chocolate chip cookies and she always enjoyed sharing them with her friends. So, after having a fun swim in the lake she was more than ready to make her cookies. Her secret recipe was from one of her best friends who lived in a little lake close to the ocean. One of the main reasons that made her cookies so special was the fact that every single ingredient in her cookies was organic.

She baked her cookies as usual. The smell of melted chocolate and vanilla was sensed even from the other side of the lake. When the cookies were all ready she put them in a basket and left her home to share those soft and chewy cookies with all of her best friends. The first stop was at Goosy Gander's place.

"Knock knock, anybody home?"

"Mmm, I can smell your delicious cookies. That must be you Duckie Cookie." Goosy Gander replied after opening the door.

"Hi Goosy, do you have time to have some cookies with me?" Duckie asked.

"I always have time for your company and your delicious cookies." Goosy responded.

Goosy Gander invited Duckie Cookie in. They both kept each other company and enjoyed some delicious cookies with some hot green tea that Goosy made. They chatted about different things, and had a wonderful time. After a couple of hours, Duckie Cookie told Goosy Gander that it was time to deliver some cookies to their other friends.

"Hey Goosey, do you want to accompany me to deliver these cookies?" Duckie asked.

"I want to take a nap right now. We can do this some other time."
Goosey responded lazily.

"Goodbye my friend, and have a nice day." Duckie told Goosey.

As Duckie left, she thought to herself, "I always get the same answer
from that lazy Goosy Gander. No one is perfect I guess." Duckie repeated
to herself. "Some people are too lazy!"

Duckie's next stop was at Turtle Tortellini's place.

"Knock knock, anybody home?"

"Mmm, I can smell your delicious cookies. That must be you Duckie Cookie." Turtle Tortellini replied after opening the door.

"Hi Ms. T, do you have time to have some cookies with me?" Asked Duckie

"I always have time for your company and your delicious cookies." Turtle Tortellini responded.

Turtle Tortellini invited Duckie Cookie in. They both kept each other company and enjoyed some delicious cookies with some hot chocolate that Turtle made for them. They chatted about different things, and had a wonderful time. After a couple of hours Duckie Cookie told Turtle Tortellini that it was time to deliver some cookies to their other friends.

"Hey, Turtlee, do you want to accompany me to deliver these cookies?" Duckie asked.

"You go ahead, and I am right behind you." Turtle Tortellini said to Duckie in a nice but a lazy tone.

"Goodbye my friend, and have a nice day." Duckie told Turtle.

As Duckie left she thought to herself I always get the same answer from that lazy Turtle Tortellini. "She never does as she promised to. No one is perfect I guess." Duckie repeated to herself. "Some people are too lazy!"

Duckie's last stop was at the Owly Wiseally place.

"Knock knock, anybody home?"

"Mmm, I can smell your delicious cookies. That must be you Duckie Cookie." Owly Wiseally replied after opening the door.

"Hi Mr. O, do you have time to have some cookies with me?" Asked Duckie

"I always have time for your company and your delicious cookies." Owly Wiseally responded.

Owly invited Duckie Cookie to come inside. They both kept each other company and enjoyed some delicious cookies with some hot coffee that Owly made for them. They chatted about different things, and had a wonderful time. Duckie realized that all the cookies were gone and it was time for Duckie to go back home and rest.

"Hey Owly, would you like to come to my place and clean up the mess that I left behind after I made cookies?" Duckie asked.

"You go ahead, and I am right behind you." Owly Wiseally said to Duckie in a nice but a lazy tone.

"Goodbye my friend, and have a nice day." Duckie told Owly.

As Duckie left she thought to herself I always get the same answer from that lazy Owly Wiseally. "He never does as he promised to. No one is perfect I guess." Duckie repeated to herself. "Some people are too lazy!"

Duckie left and headed home. She was not feeling very well. She ate too many cookies. Finally she was home and she got some rest.

The following Saturday when Duckie came back from her early morning swim she yet was not in the mood to make cookies. She had to think of something.

"I have an idea." Duckie Cookie thought aloud. "Why don't I invite my friends to come here and help me to bake cookies?"

With that idea in mind she headed toward Goosy Gander's house.

"Knock knock, anybody home?"

"Hmm, I don't smell any delicious cookies. That can't be you Duckie?" Goosy Gander replied after opening the door.

"Hi it is me, do you have time to help me to bake some cookies?" Duckie asked.

"I am very sorry but I do not have time for you today. Maybe we can do this some other time." Goosy answered. Duckie was very disappointed because she knew Goosy was not busy and all morning she would rest and be lazy.

"Well you got to do what you got to do." Duckie said bye to Goosy and headed toward Ms. T's house.

"Knock knock, anybody home?"

"Hmm, I don't smell any delicious cookies. That can't be you Duckie?" Turtle Tortellini replied after opening the door.

"Hi it is me, do you have time to help me to bake some cookies?" Asked Duckie.

"I am very sorry, but I do not have time for you today. Maybe we can do this some other time." Ms. T answered. Duckie was very disappointed because she knew Ms. T was not busy and all morning she would rest and be lazy.

"Well you got to do what you got to do." Duckie said bye to Turtle Tortellini and headed toward Owly Wiseally's house.

"Knock knock, anybody home?"

"Hmm, I don't smell any delicious cookies. That can't be you Duckie?" Owly Wiseally replied opening the door.

"Hi it is me, do you have time to help me to bake some cookies?" Duckie asked.

"I am very sorry, and I do not have time for you today. Maybe we can do this some other time." Mr. O answered.

Duckie was very disappointed because she knew that Owly was not busy and all morning he would rest and would be lazy.

"Well you got to do what you got to do." Duckie said bye to Owly Wiseally and headed back home.

On her way back she was thinking of a way to get her friends attention, and make them think about friendship more seriously. She thought of a good solution that she kept it for the following Saturday to do it.

The following Saturday Duckie was feeling good again. She baked her famous chocolate chip cookies. The smell of chocolate and vanilla was sensed even from the other side of the lake. When the cookies were all ready she put them in her basket and left her home.

Her first stop was at Goosy Gander place.

"Knock knock, anybody home?"

"Mmm, I can smell your delicious cookies. That must be you Duckie Cookie." Goosy Gander replied after opening the door.

"Goosy, do you have time to have some cookies with me?" Duckie asked.

"I always have time for your company and your delicious cookies." Goosy answered.

"I am very sorry, but I do not have time for you today. Maybe we can do this some other time." Duckie answered.

Goosy did not know what to say, and Duckie left.

Duckie's next stop was at Turtle Tortellini's place.

"Knock knock, anybody home?"

"Mmm, I can smell your delicious cookies. That must be you Duckie Cookie." Turtle Tortellini replied after opening the door.

"Turtlee, do you have time to have some cookies with me?" Duckie asked.

"I always have time for your company and your delicious cookies." Turtle Tortellini answered.

"I am very sorry, but I do not have time for you today. Maybe we can do this some other time." Duckie answered.

Turtle Tortellini did not know what to say and Duckie left.

Duckie's last stop was at the Owly Wiseally place.

"Knock knock, anybody home?"

"Mmm, I can smell your delicious cookies. That must be you Duckie Cookie." Owly Wiseally replied after opening the door.

"Owly do you have time to have some cookies with me?" Duckie asked.

"I always have time for your company and your delicious cookies." Owly Wiseally answered.

"I am very sorry, but I do not have time for you today. Maybe we can do this some other time." Duckie answered.

Owly Wiseally did not know what to say, and Duckie left.

Duckie repeated to herself that it was necessary to remind her friends that friendship is not a one way street. She headed toward the lake. The wind was whistling through her feathers, and the fresh air was touching her face. At the lake side she left her basket on the sand beach.

"Hi everyone, come and join me for a treat of fresh baked chocolate chip cookie." She yelled and invited the little ducklings who were playing in the water.

Printed in the United States
By Bookmasters